JOHN MERRILL'S NORTH YORKSHIRE MOORS CHALLENGE WALK

ABOUT JOHN N. MERRILL

John combines the characteristics and strength of a mountain climber with the stamina, and athletic capabilities of a marathon runner. In this respect he is unique and has to his credit a whole string of remarkable long walks. He is without question the world's leading marathon walker.

Over the last ten years he has walked more than 55,000 miles and successfully completed ten walks of at least 1,000 miles or more.

His six walks in Britain are—
    Hebridean Journey .... 1,003 miles
    Northern Isles Journey .... 913 miles
    Irish Island Journey .... 1,578 miles
    Parkland Journey .... 2,043 miles
    Lands End to John O'Groats .... 1,608 miles
and in 1978 he became the first person (permanent Guinness Book Of Records entry) to walk the entire coastline of Britain—6,824 miles in ten months.

In Europe he has walked across Austria (712 miles), hiked the Tour of Mont Blanc and GR20 in Corsica as training! In 1982 he walked across Europe—2,806 miles in 107 days—crossing seven countries, the Swiss and French Alps and the complete Pyrennean chain—the hardest and longest mountain walk in Europe.

In America he used the world's longest footpath—The Appalachian Trail (2,200 miles) as a training walk. The following year he walked from Mexico to Canada in record time—118 days for 2,700 miles.

During the summer of 1984, John set off from Virginia Beach on the Atlantic coast, and walked 4,226 miles without a rest day, across the width of America to San Francisco and the Pacific Ocean. This walk is unquestionably his greatest achievement, being, in modern history, the longest, hardest crossing of the USA in the shortest time—under six months (177 days). The direct distance is 2,800 miles.

Between major walks John is out training in his own area —the Peak District National Park. As well as walking in other areas of Britain and in Europe he has been trekking in the Himalayas four times. He lectures extensively and is author of more than sixty books.

JOHN MERRILL'S

NORTH YORKSHIRE MOORS CHALLENGE WALK

BY JOHN N. MERRILL

MAPS AND PHOTOGRAPHS BY JOHN N. MERRILL

a J.N.M. PUBLICATION

1988

a J.N.M. PUBLICATION

JNM PUBLICATIONS,
WINSTER,
MATLOCK,
DERBYSHIRE.
DE4 2DQ

This book is copyright under the Berne Convention. All rights are reserved. Apart from any fair dealing for the purposes of private study, research, criticism or review, as permitted under the Copyright Act, 1956, no part of this publication may be reproduced, stored in a retrieval system, or transmitted in any other form by any means, electronic, electrical, chemical, mechanical, optical, photocopying, recording or otherwise, without the prior permission of the copyright owner. Enquiries should be addressed to the publishers.

Conceived, edited, typeset, designed, marketed and distributed by John N. Merrill.

© Text and route — John N. Merrill 1986

© Maps and photographs — John N. Merrill 1987

First Published — April 1986
This edition — January 1988

ISBN 0 907496 36 9

Meticulous research has been undertaken to ensure that this publication is highly accurate at the time of going to press. The publishers, however, cannot be held responsible for alterations, errors or omissions, but they would welcome notification of such for future editions.

Printed by: John Price Litho, Brook Street, Bilston, West Midlands.

CONTENTS

	PAGE NO
INTRODUCTION	1
HOW TO DO IT	2
GOATHLAND TO BLUE BANK CAR PARK—4½ MILES	4
BLUE BANK CAR PARK TO SNEATONTHORPE—3½ MILES	6
SNEATONTHORPE TO ROBIN HOOD'S BAY—5 MILES	8
ROBIN HOOD'S BAY TO A171—3 MILES	10
A171 TO MAY BECK—2 MILES	12
MAY BECK TO A169—3½ MILES	14
A169 TO GOATHLAND—2½ MILES	16
AMENITIES GUIDE	17
INNS, Y.H.A., B & B AND CAMPING	18
LOG	19
BIRD AND FLOWER CHECKLIST	20
TRAIL PROFILE	21
EQUIPMENT NOTES	22
COUNTRY CODE	23
OTHER BOOKS BY JOHN N. MERRILL	24
BADGE ORDER FORM	26

ROBIN HOOD'S BAY FROM RAW

INTRODUCTION

The North Yorkshire Moors have always been a favourite walking area of mine, simply because of their scenic variety of moorland and coastal walking. The Cleveland Way was my first ofiicial long distance walk, more than ten years ago. Since then I have walked it seven times as part of my training programmes for my major walks. Continuing my theme of Challenge Walks—others have been in the Peak District and Yorkshire Dales—I began looking at the North Yorkshire Moors. My aim has simply been to encompass the scenic variety found in the National Park—moorlands, valleys and coastal walking. At the same time the walk is to be a challenge to complete within twelve hours, but within the capabilities of the average person. There is no time limit and the route does make a very enjoyable weekend walk of 24 miles with 2,000 feet of ascent.

The route can be termed a 'seaside bash' or 'to the ocean and back'. There is a sting in the tail, for as you head for the ocean at Robin Hood's Bay you are gradually descending, leaving the return to the moorland an ascent. I had several forays into the area trying out different paths and routes before I finally decided upon the route. In early October, I set off from Goathland to piece the whole route together. As I would be note taking on the way and since the daylight hours were reduced, I planned a weekend circuit, with Robin Hood's Bay as the overnight halt. I could not have chosen a better weekend. After weeks of rain the sun came out and enriched the glorious scene. I set off in a fibre pile jacket but soon stripped to a T shirt and shorts in the warm autumn weather. The views were extensive and, apart from a few walkers around May Beck, I had the countryside to myself. To me it was one of the most enjoyable weekend walks I had had for a long time.

I can only hope that on your walk you have equally as fine weather. and savour the variety of moorland and coastal walking. To me the first sight of Whitby and later Robin Hood's Bay were magical moments as I wove my way across the moorland and fields. Have a good walk and let me know how you fared.

Happy walking!

John N. Merrill

JOHN N. MERRILL,
WINSTER.
NOVEMBER 1985

HOW TO DO IT

The whole route is covered by the Ordnance Survey maps—

1" Tourist Map—The North Yorkshire Moors 1:50,000 Sheet No 94—Whitby 1:25,000 Outdoor Leisure Map—North York Moors—(Eastern area)

The walk is devised to be done in a single day, allowing 8—12 hours. There is no criterion to walk it in a day—it is not a competition—and if you want to spend a weekend over it, that's fine. With Robin Hood's Bay the approximate half-way point, the walk makes an excellent weekend walk. There are few facilities between Goathland and Robin Hood's Bay, both ways, and you are urged to carry enough food and water for the crossing between these places. On the outward section, Hawsker just off the route has basic amenities. There are hostels, accomodation and campsites at both ends of the walk. For those who complete the walk a special four colour embroidered badge and completion certificate is available from JNM Publications. A master record of all who walk the route is also maintained by them.

Basic Route—
Goathland—Mill Scar—Sheep Bield—Arundel Hill—Spa Hill—Lowthers Crag—Fair Plain—A169—Goathland Banks—Hempsike Farm—Laund House—Sneatonthorpe—Low Rigg Farm—Hawsker Intake Road—Raisbeck Farm—Normanby—Raw—Linger's Beck—Robin Hood's Bay   **13 miles.**

Robin Hood's Bay—Mark Lane—Demesne Farm—Park Hill—Grey Heugh Head—John Cross—May Beck—Foss Farm—Leas Head Road—Sheep House Rigg—A169—Goathland Moor—Goathland—   **11 miles.**

The whole route has been carefully mapped with walking notes, and you should have no difficulty walking round. You should always carry a map, preferably the 1:25,000 series, and be well versed in how to use a compass. The moorland crossings are short and along reasonable paths—a few are faint but the route line has features to guide you. For current details of the area information can be obtained from the:

North York Moors National Park,
The Old Vicarage,
Bondgate,
Helmsley,
York YO6 5BP
Tel: Helmsley (0439) 70657

Since the first edition of the book more than 500 people have completed the walk within an average time of 9 hours.

GOATHLAND TO BLUE BANK CAR PARK—4½ MILES

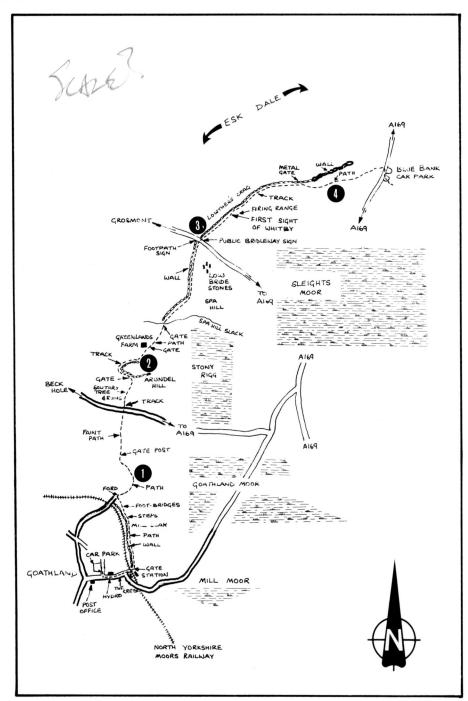

GOATHLAND TO BLUE BANK CAR PARK—4½ MILES

ABOUT THE SECTION—From Goathland you ascend onto moorland and follow its edge around Sleights Moor to Blue Bank car park, beside the A169 road. En route you have extensive views of Grosmont and Sleights before seeing the coast at Whitby for the first time. You follow either path or tracks around the moorland.

WALKING INSTRUCTIONS—From the car park return to The Green in Goathland and turn left passing the Hydro. Where the road turns sharp right continue ahead to Goathland Station. Cross the line and through the gate beyond and turn left along the ascending path by the wall, passing Mill Scar on your left before descending the steps and following the path to the footbridges over Eller Beck. Turn right past the houses and across the ford and follow the defined path by the stream. Don't take the path on your left shortly afterwards; instead continue ahead and follow the soon—ascending path with the stream on your right. This path/track soon swings to your left onto the moorland. Take the first path on your right, which is faint, and begin heading due north. The next ½ mile along here is on a faint path, but you should have no trouble, heading due north. On your left—150 yards away—are the walled fields of Allan Tofts.

Upon reaching the road to Beck Hole, continue ahead on a track which soon passes a ruin and solitary tree on your left. This tree is a useful guide when crossing the moorland ½ mile back. Keep on the track as it swings left around Arundel Hill, before turning right on its northern side and left again to Greenlands Farm. Just before the farmyard turn right through the gate and descend the moorlands edge to the stream of Lythe Beck. The path is well defined and you will see the path ahead where you ascend with the wall on your left. You keep close to this wall for almost a mile to the Grosmont Road, where there is a footpath sign. On your right are Low Bride Stones.

Cross the road and as bridlepath signed follow a track, again with a wall on your left. After ¼ mile upon reaching a quarry on your right, turn left and still keep on a track with the wall on your left. At this point you get your first view of the coast at Whitby. You keep on this track for just over ½ mile to a metal gate on your left in the wall. Beyond the wall bears left. You now leave the wall and follow a defined path across the moorland to your right to the A169 road and Blue Bank car park ½ a mile away.

DARNHOLME AND NORTH YORKSHIRE MOORS RAILWAY

BLUE BANK TO SNEATONTHORPE—3½ MILES

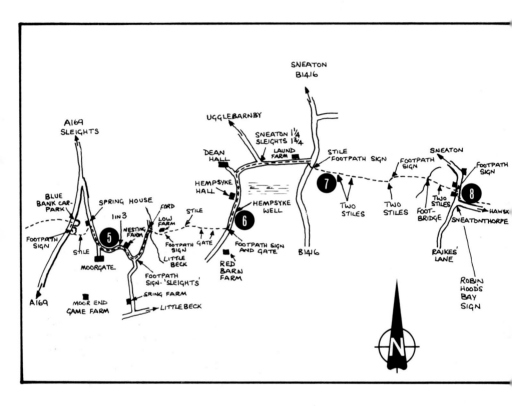

HEMPSYKE WELL—PLAQUE

Weary stranger here you see an emblem of true charity richly my bounty I bestow made by a kindly hand to flow and I have fresh supplies from heaven for every cup of water given

John Allan Hempsyke 1858

BLUE BANK CAR PARK TO SNEATONTHORPE— 3½ MILES

ABOUT THIS SECTION—You leave the moorland behind as you descend to Littlebeck before ascending to a minor road near Hempsyke Hall and well. A mile road walk brings you to the B1416 road where you cross stiled fields to the hamlet of Sneatonthorpe and the first sign for Robin Hood's Bay.

WALKING INSTRUCTIONS—Cross the A169 road to the second car-park on your right and descend a path to a stile. Continue descending but bear left to another stile close to a stream. Descend the next field to the minor road and footpath sign, beside Spring House. Turn right and follow the lane as it descends, past the entrance to Moorgate, down a 1:3 slope and past Nestling Farm. At the bottom turn left onto a tarred road, signposted—Footpath to Sleights. After ¼ mile reach the ford and footbridge across Little Beck. Just afterwards turn right, as footpath signed, and cross the field to the righthand side of Low Farm. You can walk up the drive to here. From the farm ascend directly and steeply up the valley side to a 'stile' close to the woodland. Continue ahead with the woodland on your left to a gate. Continue ascending gently, keeping to the righthand side of the next two fields to the road just south of Hempsyke Farm, where there is a gate and footpath sign. This right of way—about ½ mile—from Low Farm to the road is not used often but can be followed by basically keeping due east.

Turn left along the road passing Hempsyke Well on your right and the Hall on your left. You keep on this road for the next mile, passing the entrance of Dean Hall on your left, then a cross roads, with Sleights 1¾ miles to your left. Keep straight ahead and ¼ mile later pass Laund House on your left (camping) before reaching the B1416 road. Turn right and left almost immediately, as footpath signed, and ascend the stile into a small section of Windmill Hill Plantation. The pathline is defined as you head due east for the next mile across the fields to Sneatonthorpe. The path is well stiled and has several small footbridges. Enter the hamlet with a footpath sign and minor road and turn right.

HEMPSYKE WELL

SNEATONTHORPE TO ROBIN HOOD'S BAY—5 MILES

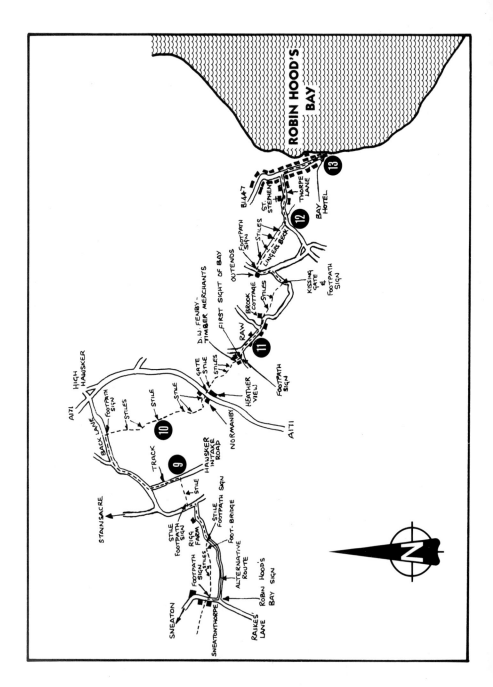

SNEATONTHORPE TO ROBIN HOOD'S BAY— 5 MILES

ABOUT THE SECTION—A mixture of field and road walking for three miles brings you to the A171 road at Normanby. A mile before you pass close to High Hawsker, the only place on the outward leg of the walk where basic services can be obtained. Just after Normanby you see Robin Hood's Bay for the first time and begin the final two miles of descent to the seas edge.

WALKING INSTRUCTIONS—Turn right then left in Sneatonthorpe and follow the 'Public Bridleway' up a narrow sunken lane. Beyond you emerge into open fields, keeping the field boundary on your right as you descend two fields, with stiles, to the footbridge across the beck. Ascend beyond to the road near Rigg Farm, via a stile and footpath sign. You can road walk this section by continuing through Sneatonthorpe to the road junction and turn left—here is the first road sign—Robin Hood's Bay 5 miles. Turn left along the road past Rigg Farm. ¼ mile later the road turns sharp left and 50 yards on your right is the stile and footpath sign. Turn right and keep the field boundary on your immediate right, to the stile. The next stile is missing and you have to straddle a barbeb wire fence. At the end of the next field you gain Hawsker Intake Road—a track. Turn left along this to the minor road, ¼ mile away. You are now heading almost northwards.

At the road turn right and follow it past Mitten Farm to Raisbeck Farm. Here the road forks but keep to the right fork—Back Lane—towards High Hawsker. After ¼ mile turn right, at the footpath sign and stile and head southwards. For the first ½ mile keep the field boundary on your right. The pathline is not defined but the route is well stiled. After ½ mile the pathline bears right towards Greystones Farm before bearing left close to the field boundary on your left to reach Manor Farm and the hamlet of Normanby on the A171 road. Opposite is Heather View— Bed & Breakfast. Cross the road to the left to a gate. Again the pathline is faint as you cross the field to a stile. Continue to the next well built stile and keep the fence on your left to the next two stiles. Cross the final field to a gate and enter D.W. Fenby timber merchants yard. Walk down the drive to the minor road and footpath sign. On the way you get your first sight of Robin Hood's Bay.

Turn right and begin descending into Raw, passing the telephone kiosk. Shortly afterwards the road turns sharp right. Here turn left, as footpath signed and stiled at Brook Cottage and continue descending first close to a beck on your left. The path is well stiled and after ¼ mile you reach a kissing gate, footpath sign and road. Turn left along the single track road. After 100 yards at the road junction turn left and ascend gently to Outends. Just to the right is the footpath sign, stile and path down beside Lingers Beck for ¼ mile to the road on the outskirts of Robin Hood's Bay. Turn left and follow the road past St. Stephen's church—Thorpe Lane—to the B1447 road and Robin Hood's Bay. Turn right and descend into the village to the sea beneath the Bay Hotel.

ROBIN HOOD'S BAY TO A171—3 MILES

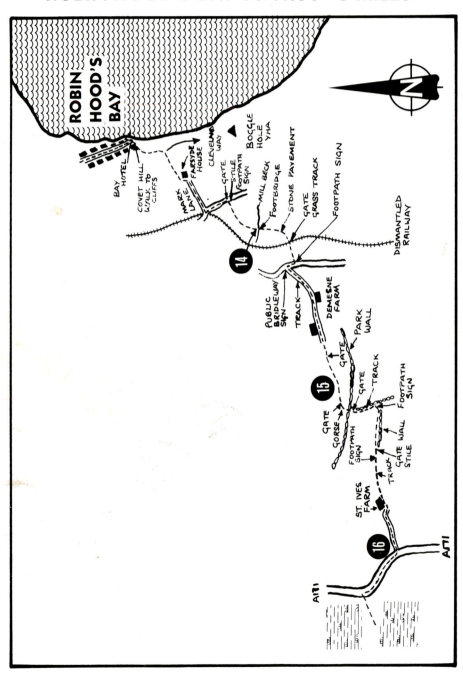

ROBIN HOOD'S BAY TO A171—3 MILES

ABOUT THE SECTION—You walk a brief section of the Cleveland Way, along the cliff tops between Robin Hood's Bay and Boggle Hole, before beginning your ascent back onto the moorland of the North Yorkshire Moors.

WALKING INSTRUCTIONS—Turn right at the Bay Hotel, following the signed path—Covet Hill walk to cliffs. After passing between the houses you descend to a wooden verandah overlooking the bay. From here you ascend the steps following the Cleveland Way. Shortly after gaining the cliff top you reach a Cleveland Way sign. Here leave the cliffs and ascend the stile and follow the fenced path on your right to Farsyde House, passing the house on its righthand side. Follow the tarmaced road from the house—Mark Lane. After ¼ mile at the road junction, turn left and follow another tarmaced road to the first gate. On the other side is the stile and footpath sign. Turn right and at first keep close to the field boundary on your right before descending to your left to a footbridge over Mill Beck. The path beyond is well defined as you ascend along the line of stone slabs. At the top bear right over the railway bridge and follow the grass track to the road and footpath sign.

Turn right then left at the bridlepath sign and ascend the walled track past Demesne Farm. Keep on this track for ½ mile. Where the track forks keep left on the ascending grass track, first with a plantation on your left before gaining the top corner of the field. Just below it is a gate and a patch of gorse to walk through before turning left to a gate in the well built 'park wall'. Keep the wall on your left as you follow a track to a wooden footpath sign. Don't go through the gate but turn right keeping the field boundary on your left as you head to a strip of woodland and a stile beside a gate. Beyond join a track, passing a footpath sign on your right. Keep ahead on the track around St Ives Farm and ascend the gravel track to the A171 road.

ROBIN HOOD'S BAY

One of the most picturesque villages in Britain, with its jumble of red roofed houses, narrow passageways and deep bay. A former smuggling and fishing village and the scene of many scuffles with the custom men. One occurred in 1779 when 200 casks of spirits were seized. The Bay Hotel overlooks the bay and the outer wall serves as part of the sea defences. In fact so close is it to the sea that on one day in 1893 the bow of the brig Romulus went through the window. The bay has seen several lifeboat rescues, the most famous being in 1881 when the Brig the 'Visitor' ran ashore. How Robin Hood's Bay got its name is a mystery but one legend states that the famous outlaw, Robin Hood, came here to arrange for some boats to take him and his men abroad.

A171 TO MAY BECK—2 MILES

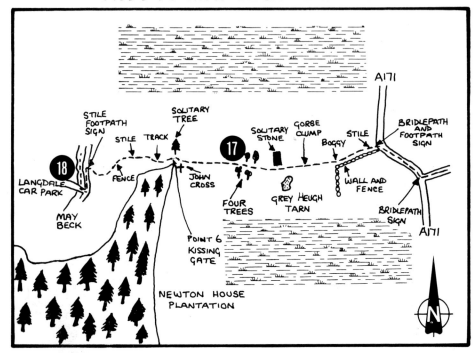

PUBLIC FOOTPATH SIGN, LANGDALE CAR PARK

A171 TO MAY BECK—2 MILES

ABOUT THE SECTION—Mostly a moorland crossing on faint paths, following definite location points to the remains of John Cross. From here you descend to May Beck and forestland.

WALKING INSTRUCTIONS—At the A171 road turn right and walk beside it for ¼ mile to the righthand bend. On the lefthand side is the footpath and bridlepath sign, a little way in. Turn left and follow the footpath to a stile. The next 100 yards is on a good path with the wall and fence well to your left. The path then becomes faint and boggy as you keep close to the wall and fence. Where it swings away to your left you keep straight, heading almost due west. First to a large solitary lump of gorse before heading for a solitary gritstone upright stone. To your left is the water of Grey Heugh Slack. The moorland is relatively flat as you head for four solitary pine trees, infront of which is the overgrown Robin Hood's Bay Road. Continue ahead for another quarter of a mile, still due west, aiming for a solitary pine tree. Close to it is Item 6 of the May Beck Trail—the remains of John Cross. Go through the kissing gate and follow the track as you gently descend. On your left is the extensive Newton House Plantation. After 200 yards leave the track on a faint path to a stile. Descend the field beyond, first keeping the fence on your left before descending to the road, stile and path sign. Turn left in to Langdale Forest and car park.

BASE OF JOHN CROSS

MAY BECK TO A169—3½ MILES

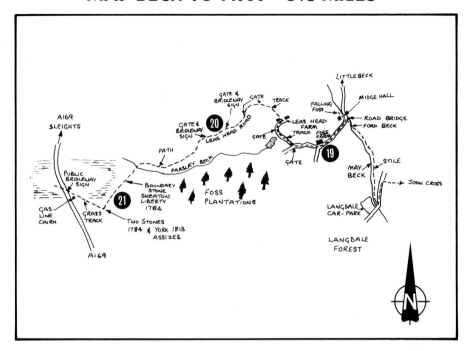

MIDGE HALL

MAY BECK TO A169—3½ MILES

ABOUT THE SECTION—First you walk close to May Beck through woodland to a track near Midge Hall. Here you can make a small detour to see Falling Foss waterfall before heading across more moorland to the A169 road.

WALKING INSTRUCTIONS—Just before the bridge across May Beck with the car park opposite, turn right on the path beside May Beck. Keep the beck on your left for the next ½ mile. Where you reach a fork in the path keep to the left and soon cross the beck to gain the road close to Midge Hall, with the road bridge on your right. To visit Midge Hall and Falling Foss keep straight ahead. Return to the road/track and ascend it. At first in woodland then on the perimeter of it to reach Foss Farm. Keep right at the farm following the track for just under ¼ mile. At the gate, turn right onto another track (the first track on your right) and follow this to Leas Head Farm, ¼ mile away.

In the middle of the farm turn left on a track but soon leave it to reach a stile in the top lefthand corner of the field. Beyond keep on a track—Leas Head Road— as you begin gently ascending towrads the moorland. The track is well gated and after ¼ mile becomes faint just beyond Littlebeck/Grosmont bridleway sign. But across this field you reach another bridlepath sign and follow a defined path across moorland. Another ¼ mile and reach the head of Parsley Beck and plantation on your left. Turn left and continue ascending gently up the moorland passing boundary stones to Sneaton Liberty 1784. ¼ mile later at the junction of tracks reach two standing stones—1784 and York 1813 Assizes. Turn right onto the grass track to the A169 road, ¼ mile away.

SNEATON LIBERTY 1784—BOUNDARY STONE

A169 TO GOATHLAND—2½ MILES

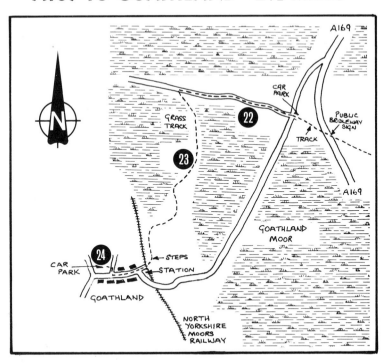

GOATHLAND STATION

A169 TO GOATHLAND—2½ MILES

ABOUT THE SECTION—The final leg of the walk with a small road walk before descending the final moorland to Goathland. A particularly attractive end admirably displaying Goathland's superb moorland setting.

WALKING INSTRUCTIONS—Cross the A169 road and walk along the track to the car park and road junction, ¼ mile away. Now you can see the beginning of the walk. Follow the descending road ahead towards Beck Hole, for ½ mile. Upon reaching the first track on your left, turn left along it and follow it for the final mile as it weaves its way down across the moorland to above the railway station. Turn right and descend the steps to the station and so retrace your steps back into Goathland.

GOATHLAND

Lying in the centre of some of the finest moorland country in the North Yorkshire Moors, the village is naturally a popular tourist and walking centre. In the immediate vicinity are several items of interest, including a particularly well preserved section of Roman road and numerous waterfalls, known locally as fosses. Goathland is on the famous North Yorkshire Moors Railway.

The name Goathland is believed to be derived from Goda-land, a Danish or Norse settlement, where Christian brothers lived. The church built in 1896 is the third on the site. The font is Saxon and the altar stone is 12th century, perhaps from the original church. The village has extensive greens populated by friendly sheep. On Plough Monday in January, the first Monday after January 6th, the sword dance by the 'Plough Scots' is performed. The dances date back 150 years and in olden days if a person did not pay up, a furrow was cut in his lawn.

AMENITIES GUIDE

VILLAGE	PAGE NO	B & B	HOT-EL	YHA	INN	REST-RANT	SHOP	P.O.	PHO-NE	CAMP-ING
GOATH-LAND	4	*	*	*	*	*	*	*	*	*
SNEATON -THORPE	8									*
HAWSKER ¾ MILE OFF	8	*			*		*	*	*	*
NORMAN -BY	8	*								
RAW	8								*	
ROBIN HO -OD'S BAY	8	*	*	*	*	*	*	*	*	*

AMENITIES GUIDE

The two main centres of Goathland and Robin Hood's Bay have numerous accommodation facilities. The following is a random selection. There are few facilities between these places, except at Hawsker which lies ½ mile off the route.

HOTELS/INNS—all provide meals and accomodation.

GOATHLAND
The Goathland Hotel—Tel. 0947-86203
The Goathland Hydro—Tel. 0947-86296
Mallyan Spout Hotel—Tel. 0947-86206

ROBIN HOOD'S BAY
Grosvenor Hotel—Tel. 0947-880320
The Victoria Hotel—Tel. 0947-880205

BED AND BREAKFAST

GOATHLAND—
Moorhaven—Tel. 0947-86224
Prudom House—Tel. 0947-86368
Fairhaven—Tel. 0947-86361
The Beacon—Tel. 0947-86236
Barnet House Guest House—Tel. 0947-86201

HIGH HAWSKER York House—Tel. 0947-880314

NORMANBY Heather View

ROBIN HOOD'S BAY Thorney Brow Farm—Tel. 0947-880036
Moor View Guest House—Tel. 0947-880576
Meadowfield Guest House—Tel. 0947-880564
White Owl Guest House—Tel. 0947-880879

YOUTH HOSTELS

WHEELDALE 3 miles from Goathland.
Y.H.A., Wheeldale Lodge, Goathland, Whitby, N.Yorks
Tel. 0947-886350

BOGGLE HOLE ½ mile from route, near Robin Hood's Bay.
Y.H.A., Boggle Hole, Mill Beck, Fyling Thorpe,
Whitby, N.Yorks. Tel. 0947-880352

CAMPING—

GOATHLAND Wyn Jackson Camp Site, Brow House Farm,
Tel. 0947-886274
Abbot's Farm Campsite, Tel. 0947-886270

SNEATONTHORPE 1 mile east of and on route at Grid Ref:NZ890065
at Laund House.

HAWSKER at Hawsker Bottoms.

ROBIN HOOD'S BAY Middlewood Farm—just off the route at
Grid Ref: NZ946046

BAY HOTEL, ROBIN HOOD'S BAY

LOG

DATE .... TIME STARTED .... TIME COMPLETED ....

ROUTE POINT	MILE NO	TIME Arr Dep	COMMENTS
GOATHLAND	0	9.30 am	
GOATHLAND MOOR	1		
GREENLANDS FARM	2		
GROSMONT ROAD	3		
BLUE BANK CAR PARK	4½		
MOORGATE	5		
HEMPSYKE WELL	6		
LOUND FARM	6½		
SNEATONTHORPE	8		
HAWSKER ROAD	9½		
A171	10½		
RAW	11		
THORPE LANE	12		
BAY HOTEL	13		
FARSYDE HOUSE	13½	2pm — 2.30pm	
DISMANTLED RAILWAY	14¼		
PARK WALL	15		
A171	16		
GREY HAUGH TARN	16½		
JOHN CROSS	17½	4pm	
LANGDALE CAR PARK	18		
MIDGE HALL	18½		
FOSS FARM	19		
LEAS HEAD ROAD	20		
A169	21½		
BECK HOLE ROAD	22		
GOATHLAND MOOR	23		
GOATHLAND	24	6.30pm	

ROBIN HOOD'S BAY PATH SIGN

19

BIRD AND FLOWER CHECKLIST

This is a random checklist of some of the more common flowers and birds to be seen on the walk. As you cross a wide variety of terrain—moorland, coniferous forests, dales and valleys. and coastline you will see a diverse range of species.

BIRDS

Moorland area—
Common Buzzard
Sparrowhawk
Red Grouse
Snipe
Curlew
Skylark
Fieldfare
Ring Ouzel
Wheatear
Meadow Pipit
Coniferous Forest
Pheasant
Wood Pidgeon
Tawny Owl
Great Spotted Woodpecker
Magpie
Jay
Blue Tit
Wren
Song Thrush
Treecreeper
Dales and Valleys
Grey Heron
Moorhen
Coot
Cuckoo
Swallow
Rook
Jackdaw
Great Tit
Marsh Tit
Dipper
Blackbird
Robin
Pied Wagtail
Greenfinch
Yellowhammer
Tree Sparrow

Coast—
Fulmar
Cormorant
Great Black-backed Gull
Herring Gull
Common Gull
Kittiwake
Guillemot

FLOWERS

Moorlands
Ling
Bilberry
Crowberry
Cross-leaved Heath
Bell Heather
Heath Rush
Cotton Grass
Bracken
Forest and Valleys—
Bluebells
Wood Anemone
Common Vetch
Common Violet
Primrose
Cowslip
Meadow Cranesbill
Red Campion
Marsh Marigold
Coast—
Sea Pinks
Coltsfoot
Sea Rocket
Common Horsetail
Sea Buckthorn
Grass of Parnassus
Wood Vetch

TRAIL PROFILE—2,000 feet of ascent

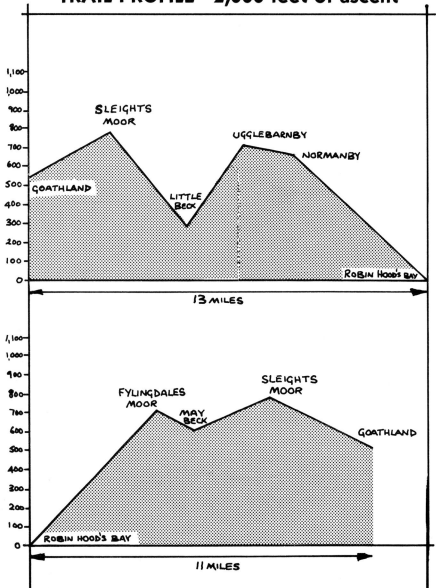

EQUIPMENT NOTES—some personal thoughts

BOOTS—perferably with a leather upper, of medium weight, with a vibram sole. I always add a foam cushioned insole to help cushion the base of my feet.

SOCKS—I generally wear two thick pairs as this helps to minimise blisters. The inner pair of loop stitch variety and approximately 80% wool. The outer a thick rib pair of approximately 80% wool.

WATERPROOFS—for general walking I wear a T shirt or shirt with a cotton wind jacket on top. You generate heat as you walk and I prefer to layer my clothes to avoid getting too hot. Depending on the season will dictate how many layers you wear. In soft rain I just use my wind jacket for I know it quickly dries out. In heavy downpours I slip on a neoprene lined cagoule, and although hot and clammy it does keep me reasonably dry. Only in extreme conditions will I don overtrousers, much preferring to get wet and feel comfortable.

FOOD—as I walk I carry bars of chocolate, for they provide instant energy and are light to carry. In winter a flask of hot coffee is welcome. I never carry water and find no hardship from doing so, but this is a personal matter. From experience I find the more I drink the more I want. You should always carry some extra food such as Kendal Mint Cake for emergencies.

RUCKSACK—for day walking I use a climbing rucksac of about 40 litre capacity and although excess space it does mean that the sac is well padded and with a shoulder strap. Inside apart from the basics for the day I carry gloves, balaclava, spare pullover and a pair of socks.

MAP & COMPASS—when I am walking I always have the relevant map—usually 1:25,000 scale—open in my hand. This enables me to constantly check that I am walking the right way. In case of bad weather I carry a Silva type compass, which once mastered gives you complete confidence in thick cloud or mist.

FORD AND FOOTBRIDGE OVER LITTLE BECK

REMEMBER AND OBSERVE THE COUNTRY CODE

ENJOY THE COUNTRYSIDE AND RESPECT ITS LIFE AND WORK.

GUARD AGAINST ALL RISK OF FIRE.

FASTEN ALL GATES.

KEEP YOUR DOGS UNDER CLOSE CONTROL.

KEEP TO PUBLIC PATHS ACROSS FARMLAND.

USE GATES AND STILES TO CROSS FENCES, HEDGES AND WALLS.

LEAVE LIVESTOCK, CROPS AND MACHINERY ALONE.

TAKE YOUR LITTER HOME—PACK IT IN, PACK IT OUT.

HELP TO KEEP ALL WATER CLEAN.

PROTECT WILDLIFE, PLANTS AND TREES.

TAKE SPECIAL CARE ON COUNTRY ROADS.

MAKE NO UNNECESSARY NOISE.

ROBIN HOOD'S BAY

OTHER BOOKS BY JOHN N. MERRILL PUBLISHED BY JNM PUBLICATIONS

DAY WALK GUIDES —

SHORT CIRCULAR WALKS IN THE PEAK DISTRICT
LONG CIRCULAR WALKS IN THE PEAK DISTRICT
CIRCULAR WALKS IN WESTERN PEAKLAND
SHORT CIRCULAR WALKS IN THE STAFFORDSHIRE MOORLANDS
PEAK DISTRICT TOWN WALKS
SHORT CIRCULAR WALKS AROUND MATLOCK
SHORT CIRCULAR WALKS IN THE DUKERIES
SHORT CIRCULAR WALKS IN SOUTH YORKSHIRE
SHORT CIRCULAR WALKS AROUND DERBY
SHORT CIRCULAR WALKS AROUND BUXTON
SHORT CIRCULAR WALKS AROUND NOTTINGHAMSHIRE
SHORT CIRCULAR WALKS ON THE NORTHERN MOORS
40 SHORT CIRCULAR PEAK DISTRICT WALKS
SHORT CIRCULAR WALKS IN THE HOPE VALLEY

INSTRUCTION & RECORD —

HIKE TO BE FIT....STROLLING WITH JOHN
THE JOHN MERRILL WALK RECORD BOOK

CANAL WALK GUIDES —

VOL ONE — DERBYSHIRE AND NOTTINGHAMSHIRE
VOL TWO — CHESHIRE AND STAFFORDSHIRE
VOL THREE — STAFFORDSHIRE
VOL FOUR — THE CHESHIRE RING

DAY CHALLENGE WALKS —

JOHN MERRILL'S PEAK DISTRICT CHALLENGE WALK
JOHN MERRILL'S YORKSHIRE DALES CHALLENGE WALK
JOHN MERRILL'S NORTH YORKSHIRE MOORS CHALLENGE WALK
PEAK DISTRICT END TO END WALKS
THE LITTLE JOHN CHALLENGE WALK
JOHN MERRILL'S LAKELAND CHALLENGE WALK
JOHN MERRILL'S STAFFORDSHIRE MOORLAND CHALLENGE WALK
JOHN MERRILL'S DARK PEAK CHALLENGE WALK

MULTIPLE DAY WALKS —

THE RIVERS' WAY
PEAK DISTRICT HIGH LEVEL ROUTE
PEAK DISTRICT MARATHONS
THE LIMEY WAY
THE PEAKLAND WAY

COAST WALKS —

ISLE OF WIGHT COAST WALK
PEMBROKESHIRE COAST PATH
THE CLEVELAND WAY

HISTORICAL GUIDES —

DERBYSHIRE INNS
HALLS AND CASTLES OF THE PEAK DISTRICT & DERBYSHIRE
TOURING THE PEAK DISTRICT AND DERBYSHIRE BY CAR
DERBYSHIRE FOLKLORE
LOST INDUSTRIES OF DERBYSHIRE
PUNISHMENT IN DERBYSHIRE
CUSTOMS OF THE PEAK DISTRICT AND DERBYSHIRE
WINSTER — A VISITOR'S GUIDE
ARKWRIGHT OF CROMFORD
TALES FROM THE MINES by GEOFFREY CARR

JOHN'S MARATHON WALKS —

TURN RIGHT AT LAND'S END
WITH MUSTARD ON MY BACK
TURN RIGHT AT DEATH VALLEY
EMERALD COAST WALK

COLOUR GUIDES —

THE PEAK DISTRICT.....Something to remember her by.

SKETCH BOOKS — by John Creber

NORTH STAFFORDSHIRE SKETCHBOOK

Badges are green cloth with figure embroidered in four colours and measure 3" wide x 3½" high.

BADGE ORDER FORM

Date completed ....
Time...
Name ....
Address ....

Price: **£1.75** each including completion certificate.

From: JNM Publications, Winster, Matlock, Derbyshire, DE4 2DQ.
Tel: Winster (062988) 454

The JOHN MERRILL WALKING BADGE is available to anyone who walks this route twice or has done another of John Merrill's challenge walks. The badges—only available to those who have walked the routes—are circular, embroidered in four colours on a black background. Price **£1.75** each.

ROBIN HOOD'S BAY

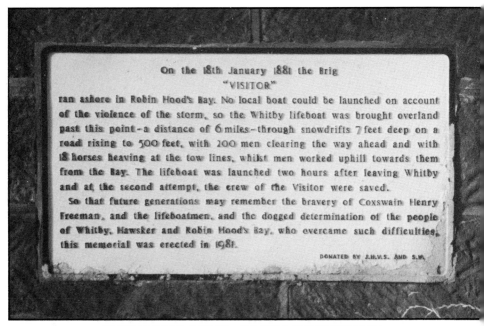

'VISITOR' PLAQUE—ROBIN HOOD'S BAY